Deer/Venados

By JoAnn Early Macken

Reading Consultant: Jeanne Clidas, Ph.D.
Director, Roberts Wesleyan College Literacy Clinic

WEEKLY READER®
PUBLISHING

Please visit our web site at **www.garethstevens.com**.
For a free catalog describing our list of high-quality books,
call 1-877-542-2595 (USA) or 1-800-387-3178 (Canada).
Our fax: 1-877-542-2596

Library of Congress Cataloging-in-Publication Data

Macken, JoAnn Early, 1953–
    [Deer. Spanish & English]
    Deer = Venados / by JoAnn Early Macken; reading consultant, Jeanne Clidas.
        p. cm. — (Animals that live in the forest = Animales del bosque)
    Includes bibliographical references and index.
    English and Spanish; translated from the English.
    ISBN-10: 1-4339-2435-8   ISBN-13: 978-1-4339-2435-4 (lib. bdg.)
    ISBN-10: 1-4339-2486-2   ISBN-13: 978-1-4339-2486-6 (soft cover)
    1. Deer–Juvenile literature. I. Title. II. Title: Venados.
  QL737.U55M2518   2009
  599.65—dc22
                                              2009008340

This edition first published in 2010 by
Weekly Reader® Books
An Imprint of Gareth Stevens Publishing
1 Reader's Digest Road
Pleasantville, NY 10570-7000 USA

Executive Managing Editor: Lisa M. Herrington
Senior Editor: Barbara Bakowski
Cover Designers: Jennifer Ryder-Talbot and Studio Montage
Production: Studio Montage
Translators: Tatiana Acosta and Guillermo Gutiérrez
Library Consultant: Carl Harvey, Library Media Specialist, Noblesville, Indiana

Photo credits: Cover, p. 1 Shutterstock; pp. 5, 13, 19 © Tom and Pat Leeson; p. 7 © Alan and Sandy Carey;
pp. 9, 15, 21 © Michael H. Francis; p. 11 © Dave Welling; p. 17 © Arthur Morris/Visuals Unlimited

Printed in the United States of America

CPSIA Compliance Information: Batch # CR111090GS: For further information contact Gareth Stevens, New York, New York at 1-800-542-2595.

Table of Contents

Young Deer 4

Amazing Antlers. 12

Built for Survival. 14

Glossary. 22

For More Information. 23

Index 24

- - - - - - - - - - - - - -

Contenido

Venados jóvenes 4

Astas asombrosas 12

Hechos para sobrevivir 14

Glosario. 22

Más información 23

Índice. 24

Boldface words appear in the glossary./
Las palabras en **negrita** aparecen en el glosario.

Young Deer

A **fawn** lies still in the forest. The baby deer's spots help it hide. They look like spots of sunlight on the grass.

- - - - - - - - - - - - - - -

Venados jóvenes

Un **cervatillo** descansa en el bosque. Las manchas en el pelaje del cervatillo lo ayudan a ocultarse. Parecen rayos de sol en la hierba.

fawn/
cervatillo

For its first few months, the fawn drinks milk from its mother. When it is a few days old, it starts to eat plants, too.

En los primeros meses, el cervatillo bebe la leche de la madre. A los pocos días de nacer, empieza a comer también plantas.

After a few weeks, the fawn walks with its mother. After a few months, the fawn's coat changes. It loses its white spots.

- - - - - - - - - - - - - -

A las pocas semanas, el cervatillo camina con su madre. Después de unos meses, su pelaje cambia. Pierde las manchas blancas.

Young deer play, kick, and leap. They chase each other.

- - - - - - - - - - - - - -

Los cervatillos juegan, patean y brincan. Se persiguen unos a otros.

Amazing Antlers

Male deer grow **antlers** on their heads. The antlers fall off in winter. In spring, new antlers start to grow again.

- - - - - - - - - - - - - -

Astas asombrosas

Los machos tienen **astas** en la cabeza. Las astas se les caen en invierno. En primavera, les vuelven a crecer.

antlers/
astas

Built for Survival

Deer are good swimmers. They often **wade** into lakes to get away from insects that bite.

- - - - - - - - - - - - - -

Hechos para sobrevivir

Los venados son buenos nadadores. Con frecuencia, **vadean** una corriente para escapar de las picaduras de los insectos.

Deer can see all around them. They can turn their large ears to hear better. They watch and listen for danger.

Los venados pueden ver en todas direcciones. Para oír mejor, hacen girar sus grandes orejas. Observan y escuchan con atención para escapar del peligro.

ears/
orejas

17

If deer find danger, they may snort. They blow air loudly through their noses. They may also stomp their feet. When they run, their white tails flash a warning.

- - - - - - - - - - - - - -

Si perciben un peligro, los venados pueden resoplar. Hacen ruido echando aire por la nariz. También pueden golpear el suelo con las patas. Al correr, la cola blanca advierte a los demás del peligro.

tails/
colas

At night, deer rest in safe places. Most deer beds have plants around them. Trees and bushes protect the deer from rain, snow, and wind.

- - - - - - - - - - - - - -

Por la noche, los venados descansan en lugares protegidos. La mayoría de las camas de venados están rodeadas de plantas. Árboles y arbustos protegen al venado de la lluvia, la nieve y el viento.

Fast Facts/Datos básicos

Height/ Altura	about 4 feet (1 meter) at the shoulder/ unos 4 pies (1 metro) en la cruz
Length/ Longitud	about 7 feet (2 meters) nose to tail/ unos 7 pies (2 metros) de nariz a cola
Weight/ Peso	Males: about 300 pounds (136 kilograms)/ Machos: unas 300 libras (136 kilogramos) Females: about 200 pounds (91 kilograms)/ Hembras: unas 200 libras (91 kilogramos)
Diet/ Dieta	plants, nuts, seeds, berries, and twigs/plantas, frutos secos, semillas, bayas y ramitas
Average life span/ Promedio de vida	about 2 years/ hasta 2 años

Glossary/Glosario

antlers: the branched horns of animals in the deer family

fawn: a baby deer

wade: to walk into or through water

— — — — — — — — — — — — — — — — —

astas: cuernos de algunos animales

cervatillo: cría de venado

vadear: atravesar caminando una corriente de agua

For More Information/Más información

Books/Libros

Deer. Backyard Animals (series). Christine Webster
(Weigl Publishers, 2007)

What Forest Animals Eat/¿Qué comen los animales del bosque?
Nature's Food Chains (series). Joanne Mattern
(Gareth Stevens, 2007)

Web Sites/Páginas web

White-Tailed Deer/Venados de cola blanca
www.nhptv.org/natureworks/whitetaileddeer.htm
Read all about white-tailed deer, and see lots of photos./
Encuentren todo tipo de información sobre los venados de cola
blanca, y muchas fotografías.

White-Tailed Deer/Venados de cola blanca
animals.nationalgeographic.com/animals/mammals/
white-tailed-deer.html
Listen to the call of a white-tailed deer./Escuchen la llamada de
un venado de cola blanca.

Index/Índice

antlers 12

beds 20

danger 16, 18

fawns 4, 6, 8

food 6

hearing 16

seeing 16

spots 4, 8

swimming 14

tails 18

- - - - - - - - - - - - - - - - -

astas 12

camas 20

cervatillos 4, 6, 8, 10

colas 18

comida 6

manchas 4, 8

nadar 14

oír 16

peligro 16, 18

ver 16

About the Author

JoAnn Early Macken is the author of two rhyming picture books, *Sing-Along Song* and *Cats on Judy*, and more than 80 nonfiction books for children. Her poems have appeared in several children's magazines. She lives in Wisconsin with her husband and their two sons.

- - - - - - - - - - - - - - - -

Información sobre la autora

JoAnn Early Macken ha escrito dos libros de rimas con ilustraciones, *Sing-Along Song* y *Cats on Judy*, y más de ochenta libros de no ficción para niños. Sus poemas han sido publicados en varias revistas infantiles. Vive en Wisconsin con su esposo y sus dos hijos.